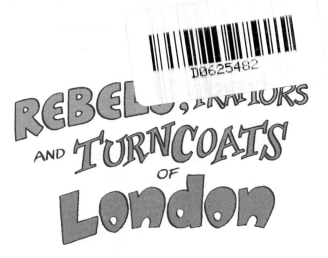

REBELS, TRAITORS
AND TURNCOATS
OF
London

First published in 2003 by Watling St Publishing
The Glen
Southrop
Lechlade
Gloucestershire
GL7 3NY

Printed in Italy

ISBN 1-904153-15-1

24681097531

Design: Maya Currell
Cover design and illustration: Mark Davis
Cartoons: Martin Angel

REBELS, TRAITORS AND TURNCOATS OF London

Travis Elborough

WATLING STREET

Travis Elborough is a freelance writer who lives in North London. He currently favours the Scooby Doo Fright Fest edition of Monopoly.

This book is for Lauren.

Contents

Introduction   7

1 A Truly Wicked Way to Go   10

2 The Peasants are Revolting   15

3 The Treacherous Tudors   20

4 What a Guy! The Gunpowder Plot   34

5 The Frightfully Uncivilized
English Civil War   40

6 Gory George and the
Terrible Traitors   45

7 Jumping Jacobites   62

8 The Gin Riots   66

9 Mighty Mary the Grandmother
of Girl Power   73

10 The Cato Street Conspiracy   79

11 Champions of Change:
The Chartists   82

12 Top Marx!   90

INTRODUCTION

Why do people betray their country? To betray your own people has always been regarded as one of the worst crimes. Traitors and rebels are feared because they threaten the stability and security of a country. In past times traitors were brutally punished. Things have only changed very recently. The death penalty was abolished in Britain in 1964. However, right up until 1999, when the punishment was finally scrapped, you could still be hanged for treason.

When friends betray our secrets or go behind our back we feel let down. Our trust has been abused. One of the most famous traitors of all time is the disciple Judas Escariot in the Bible. Judas was supposed to have betrayed Jesus Christ for thirty pieces of silver. Religion aside, this crime seemed all the more terrible because they had been friends.

You can only really betray something you believe in, or appear to believe in. Some of the traitors we'll meet here didn't think of themselves as traitors at all. Guy Fawkes of the Gunpowder Plot desperately wanted to make England a Catholic country. The peasant leader Wat Tyler rebelled against terribly unfair taxes and the top Roundhead Oliver Cromwell led Londoners to execute a lazy king!

They believed in what they were fighting for. Sometimes if you feel passionately about something you have to act. If a government is wrong you have to speak out against it. Think of men like Nelson Mandela in South Africa. Nelson was imprisoned for over twenty years for campaigning against South Africa's racist apartheid regime. He later helped dismantle the unjust government and became the country's president.

Today Britain is a democracy. If we disagree with our government we are free to criticize it and at elections vote for change. This wasn't always the case. In the bad old days you could be executed as a traitor if you even dared to criticize the king or queen!

In this book we'll take a look at those bad old days. We'll tour the capital and discover just how treacherous and rebellious old London town really was. We'll find devious dukes, terrible turncoats, revolting peasants and shifty side-swappers. We'll see how a guy with some gunpowder almost blew up the Houses of Parliament, we'll meet

Wapping's goriest judge and discover a London girl with guts, who fought for women's rights.

Mind your step, London's streets can be quite treacherous!

CHAPTER ONE

A Truly Wicked Way to Go

Kings and queens of England have always had ways of
punishing those who betrayed them or rebelled against
them. Burning, stabbing and throttling were all popular with
the Anglo-Saxon monarchs. When the Normans invaded
Britain in 1066, King William I – William the Conqueror –
introduced beheading. William also built the Tower of
London. The Tower was actually built as a royal palace but it
soon became *the* place to lock up traitors and rebels. It was
only with the arrival of King Edward I in 1272 that the laws
on treason really took off. (Off with the traitor's head, legs
and arms, that is!)

King Edward I was nicknamed
'Longshanks' because he was tall. Cranky
shanks would have been a better name for
him. Ed was a grouchy, greedy king; always
fighting against the French, the Welsh
and the Scots. When he wasn't beating
the hell out of neighbouring nations Ed
tinkered with the legal system. Ed was a bit
of a legal eagle. He invented loads of new laws
and introduced proper criminal courts. But Ed
had a nasty streak. When he had to bring in laws to punish

traitors, he came up with a pretty hideous solution. Ed decided that traitors should be hung, drawn and quartered.

Ed didn't invent this grim punishment but he made it legal and the law stuck! For the next three hundred years most traitors were executed in this way!

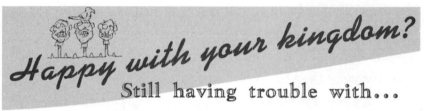

Ed had been hoping to gain control of Scotland. He'd masterminded a marriage between his eldest son, Edward, and the heir to Scottish throne, Margaret, the Maid of Norway. Unfortunately in 1290 Margaret died on her way to London before the marriage could take place!

Ed was not to be thwarted by a dead girl. He wanted Scotland and he wanted it now. So he invaded anyway and took control of the country. One frisky Scotsman wasn't happy about that. Ed could have France, Ed could have Wales but as far as William Wallace (i.e. Braveheart) was concerned Ed should keep his greedy mitts off Scotland.

William led a Scottish rebellion and defeated the English army at Stirling.

(Um ... Stirling? Stirling, Scotland? Reader to planet author! Isn't this book supposed to be called *Rebels, Traitors and Turncoats of London*? Yes, yes. I know. Just be patient, you'll see. Right, where were we, oh yes ...)

Ed managed to beat William's rebels at the Battle of Falkirk (yes, in Scotland!). William escaped but was eventually captured in Glasgow and ... (wait for it ... wait for it...)

BROUGHT TO LONDON in 1304.

William was put on trial at Westminster Hall. William was charged with treason. William claimed he was not a traitor but a Scottish patriot. He argued that he couldn't be a traitor to Ed as he was a Scot. William said Ed was not the rightful King of Scotland, only England (and possibly some bits of France). This didn't cut much ice with Ed. William was sentenced to die as a traitor. Under Ed's new law he was to be hung, drawn and quartered.

Now Ed wanted to make a real example of William – put the frighteners on anyone else who might dare to rebel against him. He decided to have William publicly executed at Smithfield. This would be like having someone executed at Wembley Stadium or Lords Cricket Grounds today. Smithfield was used for sporting tournaments and jousting contests. Smithfield was also used as a market place and was the home of the great Bartholomew Fair - it was like the Notting Hill Carnival today.

Ed had William drawn from Westminister to Smithfield by horses. This doesn't mean that a horse did a quick sketch of William. Oh no! William was dragged along the ground by the horses! William arrived at Smithfield grazed and bloody. Things were to get much worse. William was hung ... but only until he turned blue. He was cut down and while he was still alive his guts were yanked out in front of him! His guts were then burnt in front of his face. Phew! Think of the smell. He was finally beheaded and his body cut into four pieces. (That was the quartering!)

Ed was delighted. This hanging, drawing and quartering certainly taught traitors a lesson they didn't forget! So others didn't forget either he had William's head put on a pole on London Bridge!

CHAPTER TWO

The Peasants are Revolting

Life in Britain during the 1300s was taxing – especially if you were a peasant...

In 1348, just forty years after William Wallace's very unpleasant ending, England was ravaged by a ghastly plague called the Black Death. It made your skin come up in big pus-filled blisters and then you died. It killed thousands upon thousands of people. In the countryside it's estimated that over half the population died of the plague. Things weren't much better in London with plague-ridden dirty and crowded streets. The death of so many farm workers was a blow to rich country landlords who relied on their cheap labour. They responded by forcing those who were left alive to work even harder. Peasants were already treated little better than animals but now things got even worse.

At this time King Edward III was also fighting France in what was later called the Hundred Years War – whoever named it was hopeless at maths, the war lasted for one hundred and sixteen years! This war was expensive. Eddie and chief minister John Legge dreamt up a new tax to help pay for the war. It was called the Poll Tax. It meant that anyone polled or recorded as being over fifteen years of age had to pay the king three groats a year. (Groats, not goats!) A groat was worth four pence. It may not sound much now but back then it was quite a lot of loot. The king knew this was more than the very poor people could afford. He believed that richer people in each area would help by paying more. The problem was that in very poor areas there simply were no rich people. The poor were stuck with a huge bill they couldn't afford. The tax was unfair and everyone loathed it.

Eddie popped his clogs in 1377. His son Richard, who was only ten years old, became King Richard II. As Dickie was still only a youngster his uncle, John of Gaunt, helped him to rule. John was a nasty piece of work and about as popular with ordinary people as the Poll Tax – so not very popular at all then!

In 1380 John increased the Poll Tax. He also tightened its collection. He sent tax collectors out into the country to squeeze more money out of the peasants. John hated peasants. He hated their terrible sackcloths. He thought they smelt like manure. (Which they probably did!)

He thought they were revolting. And they were! Revolting against him and his tax!

During June of 1381 a gang of several hundred rebels, led by a Kentish roofer called Wat Tyler, had seized control of Canterbury. They then marched to London to demand the abolition of the Poll Tax and the end of serfdom – a law that bound a poor labourer to the land he worked on. By the time Wat reached the capital an army of nearly 100,000 rebels had gathered at Blackheath in south-east London.

Wat, together with the leader of a group of rebels from Essex, Jack Straw and a priest, John Ball, arranged to meet the teenage King Richard to discuss their demands.

Richard sailed along the Thames to meet the rebels at Greenwich. Shocked by the vast numbers he refused to land his barge. The peasants took this as a rebuff. They responded by rioting. They burned down the Marshalsea Prison at Southwark. With the aid of some Londoners they got across London Bridge and caused mayhem and murder in the city. They managed to storm into the Tower of London where they discovered John Legge – the much-hated inventor of the Poll Tax. The rebels beheaded him ... and stuck his head on a pole. (Nice touch!)

Treacherous Town

Jack Straw's Castle is a historic pub in Hampstead – the great London novelist Charles Dickens used to drink there. It was named after Wat Tyler's mate, the Essex peasant leader Jack Straw.

Dismayed by the violence Richard spoke to one group of rebels at Mile End in East London. He agreed to all their demands on the spot! A little too quickly in fact ...

Imagine the scene – there's dinky Richard surrounded by hundreds of angry peasants ... he's hardly likely to say no to their demands, is he?

'Look, trust me lads! I am your king. I may only be fourteen and as crafty as a stoat but if you just put your pitchforks down and go home nice and quietly, I promise I'll sort out this taxing stuff or whatever it's called for you. Don't worry your ugly peasant heads about the details, just run along now. You're making an awful mess of my city. I know most of you were born in barns but it's hardly an excuse now, is it? Off you go.'

Many of the rebels, convinced that the king had given his word, left the city there and then. Wat and some of the others were not so sure. They arranged to meet the king the following day. As it turns out they had good reason to be suspicious ...

On the morning of 15 June 1381 Richard, accompanied by the Lord Mayor of London, William Walworth, rode to Smithfield to meet Wat Tyler. Richard and William were surprised to find thousands of rebels waiting for them. Wat approached Richard and the pair shook hands. Richard again agreed to meet the rebels' demands as long as they shuffled off home quietly. At some point during their chat the Lord Mayor of London lunged forward and craftily stabbed Wat through the throat with a dagger!

The rebels were flummoxed. With their leader dead they weren't sure what to do. Richard bravely rode up to them and shouted, 'Wat Tyler was a traitor! I'll be your leader! Follow me to Clerkenwell' and rode off. Quite a lot of the rebels did just that. Others simply drifted away. The rebellion was over.

Devious Richard turned out to be a lying toad. He failed to keep any of the promises he had made. He then viciously punished those who had taken part in the revolt. He had hundred of peasants put to the sword in Essex and Kent. Many more were dragged back to London and hanged on special gallows set up around the city.

As for poor old Wat, his head was hacked off his body and, like William Wallace's, put on a pole on London Bridge.

CHAPTER THREE

The Treacherous Tudors

If you thought King Richard II was a nasty piece of work then it's time you met the Tudors.

The Tudors were a very powerful royal family who ruled England from 1485 right up until 1603. You couldn't trust them as a far as you could throw them – which when it came to fat old King Henry VIII wouldn't have been very far at all. The Tudors changed their minds and England's religion at the drop of a hat! Keeping up with their whims was murder!

It was the Tudors who made the Tower of London notorious as England's state prison. For most of the Tudor period no one was quite sure who would inherit the crown next. The royal line of succession normally passed to the nearest male. This was usually the son but if there wasn't a son, an uncle or even a cousin would get the crown instead. So much for girl power!

There were tons of noble families in Tudor England who

had some claim to the throne. The Tudors were in constant danger of being overthrown. They were suspicious of everyone!

Earlier kings of England had faced similar dangers but Henry VIII made things worse by dumping the Catholic Church in his Reformation.

You see, when fat boy Henry Tudor became King Henry VIII in 1509, England was a Catholic country. Henry might have been the king of England but the pope in Rome was the head of the Church. Henry desperately wanted a son to rule after him but his first wife Catherine of Aragon had only given birth to a daughter, Mary. Henry asked the pope for a divorce so he could ditch Katherine and marry his latest flame, Anne Boleyn. The pope refused. The king was all shook up. He was so livid that in 1532 he got rid of the Catholic Church in England. Henry then made himself head of a new Protestant Church of England.

He was able to marry Anne and confiscate all the Catholic Church's land and money! Henry got the girl and the gold.

Anyone who refused to accept Henry's swanky new Church was arrested for treason. He had thousands of Catholic priests, monks and nuns put to death in the Tower of London. There was a whole lot of choppin' goin' on!

One man who defied Henry was Thomas More.

Traitor Thomas

Thomas More was a Londoner through and through. He was
born and bred in Milk Street near Cripplegate in the heart
of the City and lived in Chelsea – which was then just a
village – for most of his adult life. Thomas had been one of
Horrible Henry VIII's most trusted friends and advisers.
He was the king's personal secretary and then his chancellor
– which was about the most important job in the country
back then.

Thomas was a deeply religious man and believed Henry's
plans for this new-fangled Church of England were all wrong.
When Henry announced that from now on he, rather than
the pope, would be the supreme head of the Church, Thomas
resigned as chancellor.

Henry ordered Thomas to sign an oath accepting him as
the head of the Church. Thomas politely refused. Henry
responded by locking him up in the Tower. Henry hoped
Thomas would change his mind. Thomas was not for turning.
He stuck to his guns. The pope was head of the Church, and
had been for hundreds of years. There was no need for
change. Admittedly there had been a few bad apples along
the way...

Pope Alexander VI, a member of the notoriously nasty Italian Borgia family, had been every bit as horrible as Henry. He had assassinated several

of his rivals, taken bribes and had even had a string of girlfriends ... (strictly not allowed for Catholic priests)

... but that had just been God's way of keeping the Church on its toes. The last thing that England needed was some fat bearded king ruining the Church as well as the country. No! Thomas would not be signing Henry's oath and that was that.

After fifteen months Henry was getting bored with waiting for Thomas to sign the oath. One of Henry's lackeys, the slippery solicitor general, Richard Rich, decided to act. He visited Thomas in the Tower. He tricked Thomas into criticizing the king – a treasonable act. Thomas was put on trial for treason, found guilty and sentenced to be beheaded on Tower Hill. After the execution his head was boiled in oil and then stuck on a pole on London Bridge.

On the Block

Henry didn't just execute priests and old mates. He liked to keep killing in the family! When his new wife, poor Anne Boleyn, failed to produce a son – she gave birth to a daughter, Elizabeth – Henry had her executed for treason too! Henry claimed Anne had betrayed him by having other boyfriends. On 19 May 1536 Anne was led out on to Tower Green at the Tower of London and a swordsman lopped off her head with a single blow.

Apart from getting a son and eating, girls were all Henry cared about. So Henry went straight off and married Jane Seymour. She gave him a sickly son, Edward, but lucky old Jane managed to die before Henry got bored with her.

Henry's next wife, Anne of Cleves, was so ugly that he divorced her within six months! Not that Henry could talk! He was no oil painting. (Unless, of course, it was an oil painting of a fat, fifty-year-old king covered in sores that oozed sticky pus!)

Henry's fifth wife, Catherine Howard, was only eighteen. Henry had a suspicious mind and Catherine was caught kissing a dishy young courtier, Thomas Culpepper. For a queen to kiss another man – even if her own husband was fat, old and smelly – was an act of treason. On 13 February 1542, six years after killing Anne, Henry had Catherine's pretty head chopped off with an ugly great axe at Tower Green.

Henry's nine-year-old son Edward became king. Edward VI loved being head of the Church of England. He introduced a new Protestant prayer book. Little Edward didn't get to enjoy it for long, though, as he died of tuberculosis – a horrible lung disease – at fifteen.

Bloody Mary

Edward's cousin Lady Jane Grey was crowned queen after him. She may have only been seventeen and a girl but she was a Protestant! Nine days later Edward's Catholic sister Mary seized the throne. Poor Lady Jane was declared a traitor and promptly executed at Tower Green. She was only a teenager and had never even wanted to become queen. Talk about being in the wrong place at the wrong time!

Mary set about returning England to Catholicism. She introduced a savage Treason Act, which made religious opposition a crime punishable by the state.

This allowed Mary to execute Protestants who would not convert to Catholicism as treasonous heretics.

Mary only reigned for five years but in that time she had over 250 Protestants burned at Smithfield in East London – the same spot were William Wallace and poor old Wat Tyler bit the dust! Mary was such a terrible Tudor she was nicknamed Bloody Mary.

Treacherous Town

As we've already seen, the top Tudor traitors found themselves locked up in the Tower of London. Many prisoners were brought to the Tower by boat along the Thames. There was a special gateway which led from the Thames right into the Tower. This gateway used to be called the Water Gate. Not a very imaginative name, was it? But because Horrible Henry VIII had so many people arrested for treason the gate got a fancy new name: Traitors' Gate. Thomas More, Anne Boleyn and Catherine Howard were all brought to the Tower through Traitors' Gate!

To make prisoners feel really welcome Henry had it decorated with festering severed heads!

His sixth wife Catherine Parr was luckier. In 1547 Henry died, leaving Catherine to enjoy a happy life without him!

Top of the Chops!

Off With Her Head Records presents...

KING HENRY VIII's GREATEST HITS

OVER FOUR HUNDRED YEARS OF MUSIC ON ONE DISC!

Swoon to all The King's classic smashes ...

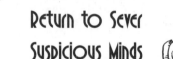

I am Henry the Eighth I am

Trouble

I Can't Help Felling My Loves

Greensleeves, Red Neck

My Old Man's an Executioner

Return to Sever

Suspicious Minds

Hardly Headed Woman

Jailhouse (Execution) Block

Heartbreak Hampton Court

AND ENJOY THE BRILLIANT NEW HIT SINGLE REMIXED BY XE CUTE:

A Little Less Conversation, A Little More Axe Action

OUT NOW!

Killer Queen

After Mary, Anne Boleyn's daughter Elizabeth became queen. Queen Elizabeth I was a feisty red-head with a terrible temper. She was a girl who loved power. She ruled England for over forty years. Elizabeth never married and so was nicknamed the Virgin Queen. A Protestant, she quickly converted England back to the Protestant religion and of course had hundreds of Catholics executed as traitors – including her own cousin Mary, Queen of Scots!

Elizabeth believed that Catholics were a serious threat to her throne. The pope had called for Catholics to rise up and depose Elizabeth (i.e. knock her off the throne). Oh dear. This made English Catholics Elizabeth's religious and political opponents. How could a Catholic remain faithful to a Protestant English Queen? All Catholics were now assumed to be traitors. Anyone even thought to be a Catholic could be arrested for treason. If they would not confess to Catholicism, Elizabeth's henchmen would torture them in a hideous dungeon in the White Tower until they did! They were then hung, drawn and quartered. Lovely!

But ultimately the greatest threat to Elizabeth's crown didn't come from a Catholic. It came from one of her closest friends.

Treacherous Town

London during Elizabeth's reign caught the deadly Black Poison of Suspect. This wasn't a real poison, it was a state of mass hysteria. Everyone was convinced that evil forces were at work in the capital! Suspicion was everywhere! Nobody was ever believed to be quite what they appeared to be ... Innocent people found themselves accused of being traitors or spies by their own neighbours! Many perfectly ordinary folk were hung, drawn and quartered as common traitors at Tyburn (where Marble Arch is now).

The Essex Rebellion

The Essex Rebellion didn't happen in Essex but in London. It was called the Essex Rebellion after the rebellious Robert Devereux, the Earl of Essex.

Robert Devereux was one of Queen Elizabeth's favourite courtiers. Bob was young, rich and good-looking. And oh how Elizabeth loved having young, rich and good-looking men flouncing about the palace. Bob was so handsome that women swooned when he walked by in his snazzy tights.

Crying babies smiled when he drew near.
Even dogs stopped barking when he
stroked them. Everyone adored Bob.
Well, everyone except the great
explorer Walter Raleigh, that is.
Walter had once been Elizabeth's
favourite courtier until Bob came
along. Since then Bob and Walter
spent their days at court plotting
against each other and generally

vying for Elizabeth's attention by wearing the most
outlandish pairs of tights that they could find. This
delighted Elizabeth even more. Two good-looking men
fighting over her, it made her heart skip a beat.

In 1599 Elizabeth decided to send Bob to Ireland on a
special mission. Bob hadn't wanted to go; he'd been blissfully
happy in London prancing about the palace in outlandish
pairs of tights. Walter was, of course, delighted! Bob
hated Ireland and Ireland hated him. He managed to make
a complete hash of his mission. Against Elizabeth's orders
he abandoned Ireland and sloped back to Essex House, his
London mansion near Temple in Holborn. Elizabeth was livid.
How dare this impudent little tyke disobey her, the queen
of England!

Bob was banished from court in disgrace.

Bob was so angry at being humiliated that he hatched a silly plot to overthrow Elizabeth. Bob may have cut a dash in snazzy tights but he was useless at plotting. Lizzie soon discovered the scheme and sent her guards to arrest him.

When the guards arrived at Essex House, Bob politely asked them in. The guards, believing Bob would come along quietly, accepted his invitation. The moment they stepped inside, Bob's own guards seized hold of them and locked them in a cellar. Elizabeth's guards were now trapped inside Bob's house. Bob and his men panicked.

What on earth were they supposed to do now?

They could make a run for it or carry on with the rebellion as if nothing had happened.

Silly Bob decided to carry on. He foolishly believed that Londoners would rally behind him once the rebellion kicked off. He was proved to be very wrong.

With a gang of swordsmen beside him Bob clattered up the Strand and on toward St Paul's Cathedral. When he got to Ludgate he found the entrance to the City blocked by the queen's troops. No Londoners had joined his gang. Bob was hopelessly outnumbered. There was nothing else for it, he had to make a quick getaway.

Bob nabbed a boat and sailed back to his house along the Thames. Elizabeth's troops were waiting for him. Bob was banged up in the Tower. Elizabeth sentenced him to death and on 24 February 1601 Bob was led on to Tower Green. An ugly axe quickly severed his handsome head from its shoulders. He was the last person ever to be beheaded on Tower Green.

Treacherous Town

The greatest playwright of Queen Elizabeth I's reign was William Shakespeare – you know, bald bloke, nice beard – who lived and worked in Southwark. Today you can see his plays performed in a replica of his Globe Theatre on the South Bank.

Will knew exactly what his London audiences wanted to see. A few choice stabbings, a love story and a happy ending and they left the theatre delirious. A few choice stabbings, a love story and an unhappy ending and they left begging for more. Add a few ghosts, floating daggers and witty jesters and Will had a box office smash on his hands!

What Will was really, really good at was plays about fiendish plots to overthrow kings and queens. Will was almost too good at them ...

One of his plays, *Richard II*, was all about the overthrow of the devious King Richard (you remember, Peasant Revolt Richard). You see nasty Richard was eventually knocked off the throne and then murdered by one of his old mates, a man called Henry Bolingbroke. Henry then became King Henry IV.

Now, when Will's *Richard II* was first performed on stage, Queen Elizabeth I was having a few problems with an old mate of her own. Yep. Our very own Bob Devereux.

Queen Elizabeth thought Will was cheekily comparing her reign to that of her ancestor, nasty old King Richard. She responded by banning his play!

The night before Bob Devereux's Essex Rebellion was set to begin Bob paid a troupe of actors to perform Will's illegal play ... he hoped it would bring him good luck. (Erm ... maybe a horseshoe would have been better.)

CHAPTER FOUR

What a Guy! The Gunpowder Plot

Every 5 November – Bonfire Night – we remember, remember a fiendish scheme to kill King James I and all his ministers by blowing up the Houses of Parliament.

The most famous of all the plotters is Guy Fawkes. The plot was not Guy's idea. Guy was just the explosives expert. The man with the devilish plan was actually the radical Catholic Robert Catesby.

In 1603 Robert had been delighted when Queen Elizabeth I died and her cousin James, King of Scotland, was made King James I of England. As we have seen, Elizabeth hated Catholics and Robert, like lots of other English Catholics, hoped that the new king would be a bit nicer. They were bitterly disappointed. Even though James was the son of the Catholic Mary, Queen of Scots, he was almost as nasty to Catholics as Elizabeth had been.

Robert decided drastic action was needed. At a house in Lambeth, he told his Catholic chums, Thomas Percy, Thomas Winwith (or Wintour) and John Wright all about his wild plan to kill the king by blowing up the Houses of Parliament. They all thought it was a great idea. There was only one slight problem. None of them had any idea how to use gunpowder. Thomas Percy and John Wright had trouble enough lighting their pipes.

How on earth were they going to cope with whopping great barrels of explosives? They decided to hire an expert. John Wright thought a Yorkshireman he knew called Guy Fawkes might fit the bill. Thomas was sent off to Europe to get him, while Robert drummed up support from other Catholic friends and relatives in England.

Guy Fawkes was a Catholic mercenary – a soldier who sells his fighting skills for ready cash – who had served in the Spanish Army and was living in what is today Belgium. Gunpowder was his game. A fervent Catholic, he didn't take much persuading to join the plot. Guy and Thomas arrived in Greenwich in May 1604. They joined the rest of the gang at their hideout in a house near the Houses of Parliament.

The plotters' original plan was to dig a tunnel from their hideout to the Houses of Parliament.

After eight months of digging there were still miles to go. Luckily in March 1605 Thomas Percy managed to hire a cellar right beneath the House of Lords. Over the next few weeks Guy slowly loaded up the cellar with thirty-six barrels of gunpowder. By May everything was in place. All they had to do was wait for 5 November – the day the Houses of Parliament would officially be opened by King James I.

Now six months is quite a long time to wait. If you start talking about what Christmas presents you want in June, people think you are a bit strange. Tell me about it nearer the time, they might say. Now suppose you had a really, really big secret. Would you be able to keep it for a whole six months? Surely you might be tempted to tell your best friend or your mum or someone ... especially if they were in danger ...

As the months passed one of the plotters started to have doubts. He became worried that the explosion might also kill Catholics who were members of Parliament. One of the conspirators – we still don't know who – sent a letter warning the Catholic Lord Monteagle of the plot.

The letter arrived at Lord Monteagle's house in Hoxton,

East London, just ten days before the explosion was due. The letter didn't say Hello Monty, there are thirty-six barrels of gunpowder stuffed under the Parliament, so make yourself scarce, me old china ... but it did warn Monteagle not to attend the opening because Parliament would 'receive a terrible blow'. The Houses of Parliament have always been full of windbags but Monty, fearing the worst, took the letter straight to the Secretary of State, Robert Cecil. Cecil was King James I's spymaster. He was a dab hand at uncovering plots and rather good at hatching them too!

Some people today believe that Cecil knew about the Gunpowder Plot months before Monty's mysterious letter. There are even those who think that Guy was a double agent who was working for Cecil all along!

Cecil quickly showed the letter to the king and then arranged to have the Houses of Parliament searched. On the evening of 4 November 1605 Guy was discovered in the cellars below Whitehall. The plot had come within hours of succeeding. Guy was taken to the Tower and lodged in a foul dungeon. The gunpowder of the plot was also taken to the Tower; it was placed in the king's storeroom.

King James himself interrogated Guy. When James asked Guy why he plotted to overthrow him Guy replied cheekily, 'A desperate disease requires a dangerous remedy!' James demanded to know who the other plotters were. Guy refused to reveal any names. James instructed his guards to begin applying the more 'gentle tortures'. These were far from gentle.

Guy was hung upside down in manacles. When he still refused to talk his body was stretched on a brutal device called a rack. It makes the bones in your back crack! After this grim torture Guy told them all they wanted to know.

Treacherous Town

Parliament Hill is on Hampstead Heath. It earned its name because it was where Guy Fawkes and his fellow gunpowder plotters were going to meet to watch the Houses of Parliament burn down.

Robert and the rest of the conspirators soon heard about Guy's arrest. Their plot foiled, they fled to the Midlands. King James's troops were only just behind them. After three days on the run the troops caught up with them in Staffordshire. Robert Catesby and Thomas Percy were killed resisting arrest. They got off lightly. Two plotters were tortured so viciously that they died in the Tower. The remaining plotters met excruciating deaths. They were hung, drawn and quartered at the Old Palace Yard at Westminster on 30 January 1606. They were executed beside the very building they had planned to destroy! (Guy, crippled by the rack, had to be carried onto the scaffold.) As a warning to others their severed heads were put on spikes just outside the Houses of Parliament.

The Gunpowder Plot is remembered in this jolly olde rap:

Ye Olde Gunpowder Rap

Remember, remember the fifth of November.
Gunpowder, Treason and Plot.
I see no reason why Gunpowder Treason
Should ever be forgot.

Not Very Good New Gunpowder Rap

There was powder in the Parliament
The Catholics wanted a new government!
Guy was in the house with a fuse
Unfortunately, this was one plot they were gonna lose.

CHAPTER FIVE

The Frightfully Uncivilized English Civil War

As we have seen, trying to kill a king or queen is an act of treason but in the 1640s the English Government itself went to war against the king!

King Charles I wasn't a very good king. He was short, shy and spoke with a stutter. (He did have a nice beard, though.) Charles was also lazy. He enjoyed dressing up in fine clothes and riding around in big coaches. He adored people bowing before him. He loved spending money, doting on his spaniel dogs and having his portrait painted. He just hated having to rule the country.

The government, led by Oliver Cromwell, were getting tired of Charles's wasteful ways. It was fed up with forking out for portraits, coaches and food for those floppy-eared mutts. They also thought that Charles's queen, Henrietta Maria, was encouraging Charles to spend even more cash. Henrietta was French and a Catholic – bad things to be in England during the 1600s.

The government politely told the king to cut back on his spending. Charles politely told them to get stuffed. He was king and they shouldn't forget it. To argue with a king was to argue with God. Charles claimed he had the divine right to rule and no penny-pinching government could take that away from him. The government disagreed. In 1642 a Civil War was declared between those who supported Charles – the Royalists or Cavaliers – and those who backed Oliver and his government – the Parliamentarians or Roundheads. No one was very polite or civil after that! Like all wars, the English Civil War was bloody and nasty.

Most Londoners sided with the government. You can't blame them. Charles ran away from London the moment the war started. He then set up a rival capital city in Oxford!

Later in 1642 he tried to regain London but Oliver Cromwell's Cockney troops thrashed his army at Turnham Green. Charles did not return to London until seven years later. By 1649 the Cavaliers had been well and truly beaten. Charles was brought back to the capital as Oliver's prisoner. He was imprisoned in St James's Palace and put on trial for... treason. Can you imagine how strange that must have been? In the past only kings had been able to charge people with treason. And now here was a commoner daring to try a king.

Oliver accused Charles of being a tyrant and of waging a

war against his own people. Charles refused to acknowledge the court. He said that only God could judge a king.

Oliver was many things but he was not a god! He had warts and was a bit of a ditherer. This didn't stop him and his Roundhead mates finding Charles guilty and sentencing him to death. They decided to chop Charles's head off at Whitehall on 30 January 1649.

On the morning of the 30th, Charles was led across St James's Park and into Whitehall through the Holbein Gate to face his execution. It was a bitterly cold day. Charles, worried his shivers would be mistaken for fear, wore two shirts. Even though he must have been terrified, Charles bravely marched up to the scaffold. A massive crowd had gathered to witness the execution. Charles greeted them warmly and made a short speech refuting Oliver's judgement. He laid his head on the block and the axeman severed it with a single blow. When the axeman held the bloody head in the air and bellowed 'Behold, the head of a traitor', the whole crowd groaned in horror.

For the next eleven years Britain was a king-free zone.

After Oliver Cromwell's death Parliament decided it missed having a king about the place. Oliver had been a miserable old so and so. England needed cheering up.

Perhaps having another spaniel-loving monarch on the throne would help. Parliament asked Charles's son, Charles, if he would like to be king. Charles, who had been living in France and Holland since his dad's execution, jumped at the chance. He had one condition. He demanded that the traitors who had killed his father be rounded up and executed as unpleasantly as possible.

The man responsible for rounding up the old Roundhead leaders was himself an old Roundhead leader! Phew! George Downing had fought against King Charles I with Oliver. With Oliver dead and Charles II on the throne George switched sides. George earned himself a knighthood by hunting down Charles's killers!

Following George's help, twenty-nine old Roundheads were tried for treason. They were all found guilty and sentenced to be hung, drawn and quartered. Their executions took place at Charing Cross on 13 October 1660.

One of the condemned, Major-General Thomas Harrison, didn't give up without a fight. Thomas was a tough, military man. After he'd been hanged Thomas was cut down so the executioner could yank his guts out. As the executioner approached, Thomas managed to punch him in the head!

The man Charles hated most of all was Oliver Cromwell

but Oliver was dead. This didn't stop Charles having his revenge. The new king had Oliver's body dug up. Oliver's putrid corpse was then beheaded and his head put on display at Whitehall – where Charles had been topped. The great London diarist Samuel Pepys recorded seeing it there in 1661.

(Almost) Samuel Pepys's Diary 1661

Flagons of ales 8 (v. bad must try to get down to 6), pipes of tobacco 4 (g.), sirloins of roast beef 2 (excellent), dishes of coffee 1 (v.v.g.). Boil under my chin (v. v. v. bad).

Humph. Head not well. Too much drinking today. Boil under my chin troubles me cruelly. Saw Cromwell's head on a pole at Whitehall. Bet that would hurt more. Maybe I'll try to close my eyes. Must sleep. V. tired. Hot date with the barmaid from the Fleet Tavern first thing tomorrow. Must try to lose four pounds before then. Oh dear.

It is believed to have been at Whitehall until 1703 when a guard flogged it to tourist for a shilling. Well, it was cheaper than a postcard. *(My brother went to London and all I got was this lousy mouldy head …)*

44

CHAPTER SIX

Gory George and the Terrible Traitors

In the last part of King Charles II's reign one London judge was notorious for his brutal punishments. During the 1670s and '80s Judge George Jeffreys was so vicious he was nicknamed the Hanging Judge. He sentenced over 300 people to be hanged and dished out thousands of grim thrashings. He didn't even let up at Christmas time! After sentencing one woman to be whipped in December 1678 he told his hangman:

to pay particular attention to this lady! Scourge her soundly man. Scourge her til the blood runs down! It is Christmas, a cold time for madam to strip. See that you warm her shoulders thoroughly!

(At least he didn't give her socks!)

Judge Jeffreys could be horrible but he was actually very popular with most Londoners. In January 1678 he helped save the city from a terrible fire. A fire had broken out at

45

Temple. It was so cold that the Thames was frozen over and it was impossible to get water to pour on the flames.

Judge Jeffreys ordered beer from the local pubs to be used instead. When all the beer was gone he decided more drastic action was needed to stop the blaze. He sent for gunpowder and blew up a house in Hare Court. It worked! The rumble stopped the fire from spreading to Fleet Street. London avoided another Great Fire.

As London's top legal eagle, Judge Jeffreys was roped in to judge all the biggest traitors of his age – and, as we shall see, he lived in treacherous times!

The Popish Plot

The Popish Plot has got the lot. Murder, intrigue, scheming liars, odd coincidences and our old friend Judge Jeffreys. Take a deep breath because this is quite complicated. Are you ready?

Titus Oates, the Teller of Tall Tales

Titus Oates wasn't a funky breakfast cereal but a devious little liar. Titus had been a vicar but he was so dishonest he had been defrocked i.e. sacked by the Church. He was a fanatical Protestant who hated Catholics. In the autumn of 1678 he visited a London magistrate, Sir Edmund Godfrey.

Titus told Edmund a strange story. Titus claimed to have overheard a group of Catholics plotting a fiendish scheme in the White Horse Tavern on the Strand. According to Titus the plotters were going to set fire to London. They were then going to kill King Charles II and place his Catholic brother James, the Duke of York, on the throne. Any Protestants who would not convert to Catholicism would be killed.

Godfrey listened to Titus's elaborate yarn. Titus had a two-track mind: killing and burning, burning and killing. On and on he went. The more Godfrey heard the more he became convinced that Titus was mad, bad and up to no good. Godfrey was a Protestant but he had some Catholic friends. After Titus had left he wrote letters warning them that this dreadful little oik was trying to drum up anti-Catholic feelings in the capital.

On the morning of 12 October, Godfrey left his home near Cornhill and went for a walk. He disappeared. Within hours of vanishing rumours that he had been murdered by Catholics began to spread. Which was a bit odd ...

He had only been gone for a short time. He could have just gone to the pub or dozed off somewhere. And why would the Catholics want to murder someone who'd tried to help them? It was all fishier than Billingsgate Market and Billingsgate

Market was then one of London's biggest fish markets so it really was very fishy indeed.

Five days later poor Godfrey's body was found in a ditch at the foot of Primrose Hill in North London. He'd been strangled and then stabbed in the chest with his own sword. The public, convinced that Catholics were responsible for his murder, were baying for blood. In all the furore Titus managed to gain an audience with King Charles II and his ministers. He told the king all about the terrible Popish Plot; the killing and the burning and the burning and the killing, on and on he went. Not all the king's ministers were convinced by his story but all agreed urgent action was needed. Londoners were seething with anti-Catholic anger. Lynch mobs and riots threatened to engulf the city.

Parliament arrested all the well-known Catholics in the city. They then arranged a series of hasty trials to convince the public that they were tough on Catholics and tough on the causes of Catholics. Five Catholic priests were hauled before George at the Old Bailey accused of plotting to kill the king. At their trial, the priests all had concrete alibis. There was no evidence to connect any of them to a murderous plot. (If a plot existed at all!) Witnesses for the prosecution were shown to be lying toads. The case against them collapsed.

But Judge Jeffreys declared them guilty anyway
and sentenced them to be hung, drawn and quartered.
Rough justice!

With Titus's help four men were then arrested for
Godfrey's murder. Only three of them were Catholics:
Robert Green, Henry Berry and Lawrence Hill. (Take note of
their surnames, they are important!) They were all servants
at the queen's home, Somerset House. The fourth man,
Samuel Atkins, was a Protestant. He was a servant to the
great London diarist Samuel Pepys! As with the priests, all
four men had cast-iron alibis. Guess who got off? Yes. It
was the Protestant Atkins. Judge Jeffreys had the other
three hanged at Tyburn in February 1679.

Here's the strange coincidence bit. Remember I told you
to take note of their surnames? Well, their names were
Green, Berry and Hill. Now, do you remember where
Godfrey's corpse was found? It was on Primrose Hill. Now
before Primrose Hill was called Primrose Hill it had another
name. It was called Greenberry Hill. Spooky, eh?

The Dense Duke and the Rye House Plot

Only a few years later there was a further outbreak of
religious plots and counter-plots.

King Charles II was a Protestant but he had spent several years in exile in France, a Catholic country. His wife Catherine of Braganza was a Catholic. Charles was sympathetic to Catholics. After the bloodbath of the Popish Plot he passed a couple of 'making life a bit easier for Catholics' laws. Many Protestants were furious. As far as they were concerned the only good Catholic was a dead one. They were even more annoyed when Charles announced that he wanted his brother James, the Duke of York - a Catholic - to become king after he died.

Charles and Catherine had no children of their own but Charles did have an illegitimate son also called James. Charles loved his son. He gave him money and a title, the Duke of Monmouth. The duke, like his dad, was a handsome lad. But unlike his dad he was as dim as a fifteen-watt light bulb. Charles despaired of his offspring's stupidity.

'Much as I love him,' Charles once said, 'I would rather see him hanged at Tyburn than confess him to be my heir.'

The duke may have been a dullard but he was a Protestant. The Whigs (they were the political party for Protestants, not a gang of hairdressers) wanted the duke to become king and not James. Head Whigs, the Earl of Shaftesbury and Lord William Russell befriended the duke. They told him what a good king he would make and generally flattered his ego.

Picture the scene ...

'So your Dad's going to make his brother king, is he?' they said in disgust.

'That's all wrong,' said Russell.

'It's a scandal. I was saying to Lady Shaftesbury only the other morning at breakfast, a son is always the rightful heir,' added Shaftesbury.

'Quite right, Shaftesbury. Why, it's against nature. You've only got to think back to evil Richard III. He nicked the throne off his nephews. It was a complete disaster. England was almost ruined. Shakespeare managed to squeeze a good play out of it, I'll grant you, but I shudder to think about it happening again,' said Russell (shaking his shoulders in a ludicrously exaggerated shuddering movement).

'And look at you, Duke, you have such a noble, dare I say it, kingly forehead. Quick, Shaftesbury, pass me your handkerchief, I feel the tears welling up in my eyes. Oh, that such a brow will not get to wear a crown. It breaks my hea–' (Russell's voice trailed off into sobs and snuffling noises).

'There, there, Russell,' consoled Shaftesbury, 'perhaps there is some way in which we could help the duke to fulfil his rightful destiny.'

'Yes, Duke, it is your destiny! Stick with us, son, and we'll do all we can to make you king.'

'I think I've just thought of a daring little caper that could get things rolling. Russell, pen and paper, I feel a plot coming on.'

And on and on the plotting probably went...

Shaftesbury's first scheme was to murder James, the duke's uncle. It was quickly uncovered and the duke was hauled before his dad. Charles forgave his son's treachery. Within months Shaftesbury, who had gone into hiding, had formed a new plan for an all-out armed rebellion. The Duke was nervous. He dithered and the plot was discovered. Shaftesbury fled to Holland. Exhausted by all his scheming he died there a few months later.

Undeterred, Russell and his friends hatched a new plot in his Mill Hill mansion. They called it the Rye House Plot. (Snappy title, eh?)

Here's the scam. Charles and his brother James both loved horse racing. They had both planned to go to Newmarket to watch the gee-gees, enjoy a glass of wine or two and gamble the odd sack of gold away. They were expected to return to London the next day, stopping off at Rumbold's Rye House in Hertfordshire on the way back into town. The plotters would hide by Rye House. When the king and James arrived they'd kill them. Simple.

Let's recap.

1. Hide by Rye House.

2. Wait a bit until two wealthy-looking blokes surrounded by spaniels and servants appear.

3. Rush out and shoot and/or stab them until they look quite unwell.

4. Er, that's it.

What could go wrong?

Well, the king did not make the journey on the expected day and so the plot was scuppered. Russell was arrested and flung into the Tower of London.

Russell was tried by none other than Judge Jeffreys. The sentence? Yes, you guessed it: a gruesome death. Russell was beheaded by London's clumsiest executioner Jack Ketch in July 1683. It took Jack three strokes to sever Russell's head. (Third time lucky, eh!)

Charles forgave the dim duke again! This time they agreed it would be better for everyone, well at least for Charles and James, if the duke went to live in Holland. And so he did.

The Mad Monmouth Rebellion
Yes, you can never keep a dim duke down! The Duke of Monmouth did return to England with quite disastrous results ...

In February 1685 Charles II died. On his deathbed – shock, horror – he converted to Catholicism! His Catholic brother, James, the Duke of York, became King James II. James promptly set about attempting, horror of horrors, to convert the country to Catholicism.

The dim duke was actually quite happy in Holland. The tulips were very pretty. He was a bit tired of rebelling. Top

Whigs from England and Scotland eventually managed to persuade him into leading a new Protestant rebellion against King James II. Oh dear.

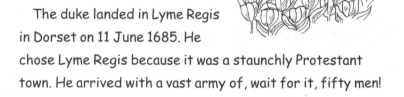

The duke landed in Lyme Regis in Dorset on 11 June 1685. He chose Lyme Regis because it was a staunchly Protestant town. He arrived with a vast army of, wait for it, fifty men!

At the same time his friend the Earl of Argyll landed in Scotland. The earl was supposed to raise troops from the tough Highlanders. The plan was for two forces: one from the West Country and the other from Scotland and the North to march on London.

The earl completely failed in Scotland. This left the duke short of soldiers. He managed to raise a force of 3,000 volunteers in the West Country. These volunteers were not trained soldiers. They were just local farmers and blacksmiths. Most didn't have proper weapons, only the scythes and pitchforks they used on the land. They were sharp and nice and pointy but hardly much use against muskets and swords. The duke made his camp at Taunton in Somerset. His supporters proclaimed him as the true King of England.

In London the Houses of Parliament passed a bill convicting the duke of high treason and sentenced him to death.

The king sent his army west to beat the living daylights out of his nephew's motley crew. At Sedgemoor near Taunton on 5 July 1685 they did just that. After the battle the duke fled to Hampshire disguised as a shepherd. He was found hiding in a ditch and dragged back to London and imprisoned in the Tower of London.

He was granted an audience with his uncle. The duke fell to his knees in front of the king's throne. He begged James to spare his life.

He said, 'I am your brother's son, and if you take my life, it is your blood that you shed.'

('Um ... but on the bright side my head will still be attached to my shoulders,' thought the king.)

James said he really was very, very sorry. However, this was the third time the duke had plotted to take the crown.

Ten out of ten for effort and all that but come on, lad. How would you feel if you really were king? Imagine it. There you are busy trying to convert England to the one true faith. Happily building a few new palaces, knighting some mates and generally trying not to fall out with France. Then every couple of years some pipsqueak pops over from Holland and persuades a few cider-drinking yokels to wave pitchforks in the air. I mean, I ask you? My own flesh and blood too! Sorry little Jimmy Monmouth but it's the chopping block for you.

On 15 July 1685 - St Swithin's Day - the duke was taken to Tower Hill for beheading. His executioner was Jack Ketch – the same man who had botched his friend Lord Russell's beheading. Gulp!

Jack hadn't improved one jot. After four blows to the duke's neck the head still clung to his shoulders. Jack slung the axe aside and grabbed a knife. He then sliced at the neck as if it was were a loaf of bread until finally the duke's stubborn head fell to the floor with a bump.

The Bloody Assizes

The duke was dead but James was worried other Protestants would try and seize the crown. He decided to punish the West Country rebels so viciously that no one would dare to attack him again. Guess who he sent to conduct the trials? Yes! It was Judge Jeffreys. Jeffreys went wild out west. He arranged for over 200 people to be hanged, some 800 transported, and many more imprisoned or whipped. The trials were thought so cruel and nasty that they became known as The Bloody Assizes. (An 'assize' is an inquest or court hearing – think of the word 'assess'.)

King James rewarded Jeffreys by making him lord chancellor.

The Bloody Assizes made James and Judge Jeffreys very unpopular. James pressed ahead with his plans to make England more Catholic. He issued a declaration giving freedom of worship to all religious groups – Catholics and non-conformists. A group of Protestant bishops in Whitehall were livid. They refused to accept his declaration. James responded by slinging them in the Tower. This made James even more unpopular.

Crowds of Londoners gathered outside the Tower to cheer the bishops as they were led away. The guards at Traitors' Gate bowed before the bishops and asked for their blessing.

Even Judge Jeffreys, who was a Protestant, thought James had gone too far! Stringing up rebels was one thing but these bishops were men of the cloth and Protestants to boot! At their trial Judge Jeffreys let them off.

Curious Orange

Parliament was now so worried about James's plans that in October of 1688 they asked William of Orange, the Protestant king of Holland to come over and rule England.

This wasn't such a strange thing for them to do.

William's granddad was King Charles I. His queen, Mary, was James II's daughter but she was a devout Protestant. The couple were cousins.

Most Londoners believed that James should go. Cockney kids would run through the streets chanting this rope rap:

> **If I had a penny**
> **Do you know what I would do?**
> **I would buy a rope**
> **And hang the pope**
> **And let King Billy through!**

Billy landed in Torbay in Devon on 5 November 1688. Billy didn't rely on West Country farmers; he brought an army of professional soldiers with him! He marched for London and was warmly welcomed along the way.

James, realizing the game was up, tried to make for France. On his way out of the capital he stopped to throw the Great Seal of England into the Thames. This wasn't a cute sea beast but a royal stamp used on official documents.

Before James could cross the Channel, he was captured by some fishermen and brought back to London. William allowed him to escape and James slipped safely away. Rather than fight on James abdicated and spent the rest of his days living as an exile in France.

One man whom James left behind was his lord chancellor, good old gory Judge Jeffreys.

With William in London Judge Jeffreys knew there was only one thing to do. He had to run away as fast as possible. He shaved his eyebrows off and disguised himself as a sailor. He went to Wapping to get a boat to the continent. He took a room in the Red Cow pub while he waited for his boat to dock. Someone spotted him and he was arrested and taken to the Lord Mayor's house in Cheapside. News of his arrest spread throughout the city. Soon an angry mob had gathered outside the mayor's house. They were keen to give Judge Jeffreys a dose of his own medicine. (And as we know this judge's medicine was anything but marvellous!) To stop them tearing him limb from limb he was taken into the Tower. Judge Jeffreys was now very ill. He had a kidney disease and eventually died in the Tower on 19 April 1689. He was buried in the church of St Mary Aldermary in the City.

CHAPTER SEVEN

Jumping Jacobites

The Jacobites were supporters of the exiled Stuart King James II. (James is Jacobus in Latin – the language of the Roman Catholic faith.) Between 1688 – when the Oranges arrived in England – and 1745 the Jacobites campaigned to get a member of the Stuart family back on the English throne.

Billy Boy Orange and Mary may have forced James into exile in France but this didn't stop the old king trying to get the crown back. James and his chums made two inept attempts to oust the Oranges. Both failed and James died quietly in France on 16 September 1701.

James's son, James Edward (nicknamed The Old Pretender) continued the squabble. He was no more successful than his dad. His son, the young 'Bonny' Prince Charles (nicknamed The Young Pretender so people didn't get confused) had more luck but not much. In August 1745 he landed in the Scottish Highlands. By September he had gained control of Edinburgh, the Scottish capital. He was now Master of Scotland.

Edinburgh is hundreds of miles from London but news of

Bonny Prince Charles's invasion caused panic in the English capital. A state of emergency was declared. Troops were placed on Finchley Common. Local constables and city warders prowled the streets looking for suspicious characters. (Anyone in tartan was arrested!) London waited with bated breath for the Jacobite rebels to arrive.

The invasion of London never happened. In April 1746 English troops crushed Charles's Jacobite army at the very bloody Battle of Culloden, near Inverness.

Some Jacobite soldiers were dragged down to London and put on trial for treason in Southwark on 30 July 1746. Surprise, surprise, they were all found guilty. As a warning to others they were publicly beheaded and then disembowelled on Kennington Common. I bet they were gutted!

The following year one of the top Jacobites, Simon Fraser the Laughing Lord Lovat, was topped at the Tower of London.

Simon was captured just after the Battle of Culloden and taken to the capital. To make an example of him, the government paraded Simon through the streets of London before locking him in the Tower.

As his cart trundled along, one old woman cried out, 'you'll get that nasty head of yours chopped off, you ugly old Scotch dog.' To which Simon laughed and replied charmingly, 'I believe I shall, you ugly old English hag.' (People were so polite in the old days!)

At his trial Simon laughed at the judge and generally misbehaved. He was found guilty of high treason and sentenced to death by beheading. On the morning of 9 April 1747 Simon was led out on to Tower Hill to be executed. An enormous crowd had gathered to watch him get the chop. The crowd was so big that some bright spark carpenter had hastily built a viewing platform by the Ship Tavern nearby. As Simon climbed the scaffold, the crowd on the platform strained to get a better view. The platform collapsed! Ten people including the carpenter who'd built it died instantly.

Simon giggled and shouted, 'The more mischief, the

better sport.' He cheerfully joked with the executioner and even tested the axe to see if it was sharp enough. He lay his head on the block and gave a final guffaw just before the blade hit his neck. He laughed his head off.

As it turned out Simon, the laughing lord, had the last laugh. He was the last person to be beheaded on Tower Hill.

CHAPTER EIGHT

The Gin Riots

We have seen treason over religion and rebellions over taxation. However, some of the worst riots ever seen in London occurred over plans to restrict the sale of a drink ... (and no, it wasn't Sunny Delight!)

When William of Orange and Mary were on the throne, things in England went Dutch. One Dutch delicacy to really take off was the drink Geneva, or 'gin' as it came to be called. It first arrived in London from Holland in the 1690s.

By the 1720s it was London's favourite tipple. In its day it was far bigger than Cola or Tango combined. In 1727 over 3,500,000 gallons of the stuff was drunk. In some London parishes one house in five was a gin shop. You couldn't move for gin shops. It was worse than Starbucks now! By 1735 a staggering 5,500,000 gallons were being guzzled. Things were getting out of hand.

It was particularly popular with the poor. Gin was cheaper than beer and wine. And getting drunk was one way of escaping the hideousness of slum life. Shops proudly displayed signs that read:

Drunk for One Penny
Dead Drunk for Two
Clean Straw for Nothing!

(You lay on the straw to sleep off your hangover. It was a rough bed for a sore head.)

In those days medicine was still very primitive. Gin was seen as a tonic and even used as kind of anaesthetic. Women, in particular, used it to cope with rearing children. It was nicknamed Mother's Ruin.

Almost anyone could distil and sell gin. In the poor areas of London such as St Giles and Holborn vendors roamed the streets flogging cheap gin off the back of carts. Today you have to be eighteen years of age to buy alcoholic drinks. In the 1700s there were no age limits. Most gin shops had stools by their counters so children could sup at the bar!

In 1729 the government, worried about the craze for gin, introduced new laws. If you wanted to sell gin you now had to pay the government £20 for a license. They also introduced a tax of two shillings for every gallon of gin sold. This was supposed to halt the explosion of gin drinking. It failed. Gin selling went underground. Illegal gin shops sprang up over London. The quality of gin declined rapidly. Some illegal gin was so bad that it was poisonous. People really were dead drunk! They were drinking themselves to death.

The Whig government, led by Robert Walpole – Britain's very first prime minister – decided tougher measures were needed. Robert drafted a 'let's make it really very hard indeed for people to sell or buy gin' act. His Gin Act made gin virtually illegal. The act was passed on 5 May 1736 but wasn't due to become law until September, three whole months later.

London gin sellers and gin drinkers were angry about the new law. It hit them where it really hurt: in their pockets.

Under the new law gin sellers would have to pay a small fortune to sell the drink and gin drinkers would have to pay much, much more for their tipple.

Robert's political opponents, the Jacobites (originally supporters of King James II) and the Tories (who are still a political party today) saw a chance to gain power. They launched a campaign against the government. Their message was simple: 'Vote for the Whigs and Lose Your Gin'

That summer London was rocked by a series of gin riots. Distillers keen to stop the law gave out free gin to crowds of protesters. In June and July drunken mobs went on the rampage in Spitalfields and Shoreditch and in Lambeth and Southwark. On the day before the act was due to become law, dealers gave away vast quantities of gin. They claimed it was to celebrate the new Gin Act – which they nicknamed Madam Geneva's Lying in State. Secretly they hoped a riot would scupper the Gin Act and bring the government down.

The government, fearing the worst, wisely stationed armed guards throughout the city. Soldiers marched along Chancery Lane and the cavalry paraded around Whitehall and in Covent Garden. (Imagine today just how you would feel if you saw tanks driving across Leicester Square, or armed soldiers marching on Oxford Street!)

A doll in the image of Madame Geneva was paraded through the city by a mob but with so many soldiers around their protest passed relatively peacefully.

In the end Robert's Gin Act was no more use against gin drinking than the previous law. The public hated the excise men whose job it was to collect the new taxes and licenses. Snooping excise men were often beaten up or even murdered. There was no proper police force to help them and so the act was simply ignored.

Gin drinking became an even bigger problem. Over the next six years gin production rose by nearly 50 per cent. Eight million gallons of the stuff were drunk in 1740 alone. That's the same as 64 million pints of milk. In 1743 the government decided enough was enough and tried to introduce a new gin act. Once again violent riots broke out in London. This time the government pressed on. By 1751 new measures were in place. Gin was heavily taxed and its sale was strictly controlled. There was an instant slump in gin drinking. The new act was a success. It also made the government a few extra quid as well! Spirits have been taxed in this way ever since.

Treacherous Town

The Poisoned Pop Gun Plot

King George III was mad. He wasn't angry, he really was mad. He had an illness called porphyria, which sent him a bit bonkers. In May 1796 London was rocked by news of an attempt to kill George that was even more insane than the king himself.

On 11 May 1796 four men, Robert Crossfield, Paul Thomas, John Smith and George Higgins appeared at the Old Bailey law courts charged with treason. They were accused of plotting to kill the king.

'No change there,' I hear you cry. I know we've already read about dozens of people who have tried to do that but ... so far none of them have attempted to use a popgun that fired poisoned darts!

Interesting stuff, eh?

Sorry folks but despite a snappy title the Poisoned Popgun Plot is perhaps the dullest story in this book. (I'd skip it if I were you.

There some great stuff on the Cato Street Conspiracy later.)

You see, the men were actually arrested for trying to buy, wait for it, a long brass pipe at a blacksmith's shop in Cock Lane in the City. The blacksmith – who must have been as bonkers as King George – became convinced that the men were up to no good. He rather strangely believed that they wanted to use the pipe to make a gun to shoot poison darts at the king. This metal man was obviously mental. None of the men had any poison or darts but later they were all arrested and taken to Newgate Prison.

At the trial the case against them collapsed. The Poison Popgun Plot popped. (Don't say I didn't warn you. I told you it was dull! But at least it was short.)

CHAPTER NINE

Mighty Mary the Grandmother of Girl Power

Around the time London was recovering from the gin craze a remarkable and rebellious little girl was born. Mary Wollstonecraft was born in Spitalfields in East London in 1759. When Mary was growing up, girls were expected to look gentle and fluffy. They were told to keep quiet and not to argue with boys. Little girls were made of sugar and spice and all things nice. Little boys, now they were allowed to shout and fight, climb trees and play with snakes, snails and puppy dog tails. (No one bothered to ask the puppy dogs what they thought about this!) Now Mary was different. She was a rebel. She didn't see that just because she was a girl she should keep quiet or miss out on all the fun of playing with puppy dogs' tails!

Mary was feisty and clever. She became a teacher and at the age of twenty-five she was running a school in Newington Green with her sister, Eliza. In those days hardly any girls got an education. Even if girls did go to school they were usually only taught the basics: how to read and write and if they were really, really lucky how to do some needlework. Mary thought this was outrageous. Girls' brains were just as a good as boys – perhaps even better! At her school she taught girls a range of subjects and she encouraged them to think for themselves.

Her ideas on education were radical and exciting. In 1786 she met the London publisher, Joseph Johnson. Joseph was London's top book dog.

Joseph published some of the greatest writers of all time. He published poems by William Blake and Samuel Taylor Coleridge. He published essays by the radical thinker William Godwin. (We'll hear more about him in a bit). He published Thomas Paine's revolutionary book *The Rights of Man*. In the 1780s Joseph's bookshop in St Paul's Churchyard was the best in London.

Joseph was impressed by Mary's ideas. He asked her to write a book about education. Her book, *Thoughts on the Education of Girls*, was published in May 1786. It caused shockwaves and made Mary's name.

Sorry, we have to leave London for a bit. You see, across the channel in France, a revolution was brewing.

Revolting Times

Most ordinary French people depended on bread as their main food. In the autumn of 1788 poor weather destroyed crops of wheat and barley – the ingredients used in making bread. There was a massive shortage of bread. The price of bread rocketed. Poor people in Paris just couldn't afford to buy it. They began to starve.

While the poor starved, the king of France, Louis XVI, and his queen, Marie Antoinette, lived in luxury in a gigantic palace called Versailles on the edge of the city. When Queen Marie Antoinette was told the poor didn't have any bread she is rumoured to have joked: 'Let them eat cake!' This probably didn't happen but the poor were so sick of the queen and her lazy husband they were happy to believe it.

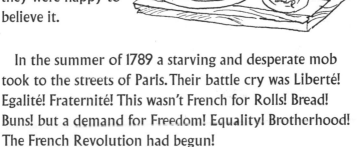

In the summer of 1789 a starving and desperate mob took to the streets of Paris. Their battle cry was Liberté! Egalité! Fraternité! This wasn't French for Rolls! Bread! Buns! but a demand for Freedom! Equality! Brotherhood! The French Revolution had begun!

On 14 July 1789 the mob stormed into the Bastille prison. The Bastille, like the Tower of London, was a symbol of the king's power. After the mob had freed all the prisoners and made off with its stores of gunpowder, they headed off to Versailles. The mob smashed into the royal palace and led the king and queen away. They were imprisoned in the centre of Paris. France declared itself a republic – a king-free country! A young lawyer called Maximilien Robespierre and members of the army took charge.

Back in London Mary was inspired by the French Revolution. She wrote another book, *A Vindication of the Rights of Man*, praising the revolution and calling for the abolition of the monarchy in England.

The writers Tom Paine and William Godwin – both fans of the French Revolution – thought this book was absolutely brilliant. Mary, William and Tom soon became good friends and met regularly to talk about politics.

In 1792 Mary published her most famous book, *A Vindication of the Rights of Women*. In it she boldly argued for equal rights for women. Her ideas were truly revolutionary! Many male critics hated the book. They called Mary a 'hyena in petticoats'. Mary didn't care, she knew she was right!

In 1793 Mary moved to Paris to lend her support to the new French Republic. She was disappointed with what she found there.

In January 1793 Robespierre's government had executed King Louis. They chopped his head off with a device called a guillotine. Oh, how Robespierre and his mates loved the guillotine! Over the next year they used it to execute over 3,000 aristocrats in Paris alone! It was known as The Reign of Terror. The revolution was supposed to bring freedom and equality. Instead a brutal military government fond of executing its own citizens was in power!

No one was safe. In August 1794 Robespierre himself was arrested! He was tried for treason and guillotined! The man at the top got the chop!

Mary returned to London and devoted herself to campaigning for women's rights. She discussed many of her new ideas with William Godwin. Gradually the pair fell in love and married in March 1797. Mary gave birth to a sparky little daughter whom they called Mary. Sadly disinfectant and antiseptics had not yet been invented and Mary

Wollstonecraft caught an infection during the birth. The grandmother of girl power died on 10 September 1797.

Mary and William's daughter, Mary Godwin, inherited her parents' brains. She later married the poet Percy Shelley and went on to write the horror classic *Frankenstein*!

CHAPTER TEN

The Cato Street Conspiracy

Streets can be crowded or poorly paved but they are rarely rebellious. Cato Street is no exception. In the early 1800s it was as well behaved as any other street in London. Its buildings and paving slabs had never plotted to kill a king or take over the country. (How many bricks ever have?) However, in 1820 a house on Cato Street was the secret hideout of a gang of revolutionaries who planned to assassinate the entire government.

The man behind the plan was Arthur Thistlewood. Arthur had once been a soldier, a lieutenant in charge of a small group of men. He got to wear a smart uniform with bright shiny buttons on it and to bark orders from dawn until dusk. He'd been happy. When his army career ended Arthur bought a farm in Horncastle, Lincolnshire, but found he missed arranging daring missions and barking orders. He particularly missed his shiny-buttoned uniform.

He moved to London and got involved with a political group with a snazzy name – the Spencean Philanthropists – instead. Most of the Spenceans were dedicated to making England a fairer country. They believed in equality and advocated free education for all. A few Spenceans had more radical ideas. Guess who had the most radical ideas of all? Yep, it was Arthur. He believed that there was only one way to change how England was governed and that was to remove the government – using violence if necessary.

In 1816, Arthur cooked up an elaborate scam. The Spenceans had organized a protest meeting to take place at Spa Fields, Islington, on 2 December. Arthur hoped to engineer a riot at the meeting. While the police were busy arresting the rioters, a crack team led by Arthur would seize control of the Tower of London and the Bank of England.

However, a government spy, John Castle, had secretly joined the Spenceans and got wind of the plan and Arthur found himself in gaol. At his trial there was little hard evidence against him and so he was let off.

Arthur was free to plot another day. Which is exactly what he did. Unfortunately Arthur didn't realize that one of his closest men, George Edwards, was also a government spy.

George led Arthur into a trap. He showed Arthur a newspaper article which announced that most of the cabinet - the ruling elite of the government - were going to a posh dinner at a house in Grosvenor Square on 23 February 1820. Within seconds Arthur had dreamt up a ridiculous plot to kill off the cabinet as they sat waiting for their puddings to arrive.

In fact on 23 February the cabinet would be nowhere near Grosvenor Square, the story of the meal had been placed in the newspaper by the government. It was bait to lure Arthur out into the open. With a nudge from George he'd fallen for it hook, line and sinker.

After many months of feverish preparations 23 February arrived. Arthur and his gang were holed up in a house close to Grosvenor Square on nearby Cato Street. Armed with guns and hand grenades they sat nervously waiting to storm the dinner. Imagine their surprise when thirteen policemen suddenly burst in on their hideout and apprehended them. Arthur refused to come quietly and as he scuffled to escape his pistol went off, killing a young policeman. He was wrestled to the ground and then bound and gagged and dragged off to Newgate Prison.

He was found guilty of high treason and hanged outside the gaol on 1 May 1820.

CHAPTER ELEVEN

Champions of Change: The Chartists

The Cato street gang weren't the only people trying to change the world. Everything was changing in Britain during the early 1800s. New technology transformed how people lived and worked. Steam trains and factories replaced coaches and traditional cottage industries. This was a revolution – The Industrial Revolution.

The greatest changes occurred in the Midlands and the north of England, around cities such as Birmingham and Manchester. The Industrial Revolution created a new working class. This new class of industrial workers included men, women, and even small children who worked in cotton mills, pottery works and coal mines.

Often skilled workers – such as weavers and potters – were forced to take dull factory jobs as machines began to mass produce the products formerly made by hand. Wages were low, hours were long, and working conditions horrible and dangerous.

London was not a new industrial city but many of its traditional industries were devastated by the changes sweeping the nation. Weavers in Spitalfields – who used handlooms – found it impossible to compete against factory looms, which could produce vast quantities of cheap cloth.

Ordinary workers seemed unable to stop the changes or be able to fight for better wages and conditions. Most ordinary people were not entitled to vote. The government didn't appear to care about them. It only seemed interested in helping the rich factory owners and businessmen make even more money. (No change there then!) You had to be a property owner to become a member of parliament. MPs did not receive wages, so you usually had to be rich to become an MP in the first place. Many MPs were corrupt and took bribes to change the law and feather their nests.

The areas each MP represented varied in size. This meant that some MPs gained their seats with only a handful of votes. At Dunwich in Suffolk in 1831 only thirty-two people could vote! Old Sarum in Wiltshire was even smaller. It had just three houses. Of a massive population of fifteen people only eleven of them were entitled to vote. Towns like these were prime targets for corruption. Anyone

wanting to become an MP only needed to bribe a couple of locals to vote for him and bingo! They were elected as the Right Horrible, sorry, Honourable Member of Parliament for Crooked Fiddlington!

These areas were so notorious they were nicknamed Rotten Boroughs.

In London three men – William Lovett, Francis Place and Henry Hethington – thought this was all wrong and formed a society to fight for political change. They called themselves The London Working Men's Association. They wrote pamphlets and published newspapers calling for action.

In 1819 the government, worried about hostile criticism of its policies, had tried to control the press by introducing a tax on newspapers. Any newspaper that did not bear a government stamp was illegal. Instead of killing off newspapers the tax actually encouraged an underground press.

One of the most popular unstamped papers was published by Henry 'London Working Men's Association' Hethington. Henry was a London printer who slyly produced his *Poor Man's Guardian* newspaper in the back room of his printshop. Priced at 1 pence it sold over 16,000 copies a week!

The London Working Men's Association wasn't the only group calling for political change. There were similar groups all across the country. However, as London was home to the national government it was central to what became known as the Chartist Movement.

'A demonstration in the streets of London comes before the eyes of those who make the laws' was how one bright Chartist spark put it at the time. (Thanks for that, Mr Chartist! I couldn't have put it better myself ... er, which is why haven't even bothered to try!)

In 1838 William Lovett drafted a petition calling for six changes to the law. He called it the People's Charter.

The People's Charter (or All I Want for Christmas Is the Right to Vote)

Dear Father Government,

We have been good all year. Honest! You can ask our parents! We have all worked really, really, really hard too. It would be great if this Christmas you could brings us some lovely presents from your big woolsack. There are only six things in the whole wide world we want! (They are listed below.) Please, please, please, Father Government, if you fix this for us we promise to tidy our bedrooms up and make our beds every morning for the next year. Cross our hearts and hope to die if we are lying! We won't ask for anything else all year, promise. Not even on our birthdays!

Love
The People

P. S. We've left the Speaker of the House a nice saucer of milk! We thought he might be thirsty after shouting 'Order, order' all day long.

What we want!

1. Votes for All Men

2. Proper electoral districts to end Rotten Boroughs

3. Men who don't own houses should be allowed to become MPs anyway

4. Wages for MPs

5. Annual General Elections

6. A Secret Ballot

(Eagle-eyed readers might have spotted that they asked for votes for all men … but not women! Now what would Mary Wollstonecraft have made of that!)

William and campaigners all over England gathered over one and a quarter million signatures supporting the charter. In 1839 a national Chartist convention was held in London and the charter was presented to the House of Commons. A vote was called in Parliament but the MPs rejected the charter. (Only 46 MPs supported the charter while 235 MPs voted against it.)

Many Londoners were bitterly disappointed and some rioted in the streets. The Chartists vowed to continue their campaign. Three years later they presented another petition to the government. This one had a staggering three million signatures on it! Again the government rejected the charter.

In April 1848, nine years after the first charter had been presented to Parliament, the Chartists organized huge demonstrations on Kennington Common in South London and at Trafalgar Square. They hoped that this might, finally, persuade the government to change its mind.

Treacherous Town

Trafalgar Square has long been the place for public meetings and demonstrations. On 13 November 1887 a meeting held by one political group, the Socialist Democratic Federation, got out of hand. The government had banned the meeting. The police were ordered to stop the marchers entering Trafalgar Square. A conflict broke out between the marchers and the police. Two protesters died in the skirmish. This grim event became known as Bloody Sunday (not to be confused with the Bloody Sunday of Northern Ireland).

The government was terrified. The Duke of Wellington – you know, the bloke who beat Napoleon at Waterloo and who invented wellies – was put in charge of keeping order in the city. He positioned armed troops on Blackfriars Bridge – the bridge the Chartists planned to use to cross the Thames.

The day of the demonstration arrived ... it poured down with rain! A large crowd gathered at Kennington but the terrible weather had put loads of people off. The Chartists' great demonstration was a wash-out. The bedraggled demonstrators peacefully made their way to Parliament and once again presented their petition. Third time lucky, eh? Er no. The government rejected the charter.

The Chartists had failed and the movement fizzled out. But their ideas did not die. Most of their demands were eventually met in two reform acts passed just a few years later, in 1867 and 1884.

Only one of their six demands never became law. Can you guess which one it was?

It was number 5 - the call for annual general elections. British government is allowed to sit for five years before calling an election!

CHAPTER TWELVE

Top Marx!

Karl Marx was a thinker whose ideas – like the Chartists – really did change the world. Karl thought that the world was divided in to two groups or classes. The wealthy people who owned businesses – whom he called capitalists – and the poor who were forced to work for them – whom he called the proletariat. He believed that as the rich got richer, the poor proletariats would rebel and create a new society where everyone was equal. He called this Communism. His ideas inspired the Russian Revolution in 1914. Sadly the Russian Revolution didn't result in a more equal society. Until 1989 Russia and most of Eastern Europe (what was known as the Soviet Block) was ruled by a brutal totalitarian regime.

Karl may have been wrong about revolutions but his writings about economics – how business and money works – are still read today.

Karl was born in Germany in 1818 – just a year before Queen Victoria's birth. His revolutionary ideas got him into trouble in Germany. In 1849 at thirty-one years of age he moved his family to London. He lived in London until his death in 1883.

When Karl, his wife Jenny and their children first arrived in the capital they were very poor. The whole family lodged in one grubby room in Dean Street in Soho.

This was a terrible time for the Marxes. Three of their children died in Dean Street. Marx tried to support his family by writing journalism. This wasn't well paid. At one point Karl tried to get a job as a clerk with the railways. He was rejected because he had terrible handwriting!

Luckily Karl's best friend Friedrich Engels was wealthy and generously gave them money to live on. This allowed Karl to devote most of his time to studying in the British Museum's famous round Reading Room! (You can visit the old Reading Room at the museum today.)

Even though Karl didn't have a proper job he was the leader of a radical group called The International Working Men's Association.

In 1856 Jenny inherited some money and the family moved to a nice house in Kentish Town. It was here that Karl started worked on his most famous book, *Capital*.

Karl wasn't a dull bookworm. He was a big jovial chap with a huge beard and a mane of thick hair. He adored his wife and children. When not reading or writing Karl liked to stroll on

Hampstead Heath. He enjoyed smoking cigars and loved drinking beer in pubs in Hampstead and Highgate. One of his favourite pubs was the Jack Straw's Castle at Hampstead. (You remember it was named after the Revolting Peasant Jack Straw!)

Karl may have been a revolutionary thinker but he was a respected figure in his neighbourhood. In 1868 he was even asked to help on the local Neighbourhood Watch scheme of the day!

In 1874 Karl was so happy with life in London that he applied to become an English citizen. He was turned down! The Home Office described him as 'a notorious German agitator who had not been loyal to his own king and country'.

Karl the Kentish Town father of communism died on 14 March 1883. He was buried at Highgate cemetery on 17 March 1883. At the time of his death hardly any of his books had been published. Karl died poor and unknown. Only eleven people attended the ceremony. His mate Friedrich Engels proudly boasted that Karl's name and work would 'endure through the ages'. He turned out to be right after all! Thousands of people visit his grave at Highgate every year.

I hope you've enjoyed our tour through the capital's rebellious roads and treacherous streets.

Nowadays we are allowed the freedom of expression that most of the earlier inhabitants of London were denied. If we go on a protest march through Hyde Park against a government policy we are exercising our rights as citizens and will not be condemned as traitors. Parliament protects our right to protest, however much it annoys the government. However, we can still be prosecuted for treason if we betray the country of which we are a citizen - for example, by selling military secrets to a foreign power.

You can see from some of the rebellious tales in this book that our freedom to express our opinions or to practise any religion we choose, has been a long time coming and hard won, and the citizens of London are not about to give it up in a hurry!

Other books from Watling St you'll love

CRYPTS, CAVES AND TUNNELS OF LONDON
By Ian Marchant
Peel away the layers under your feet and discover the unseen treasures of London beneath the streets.
ISBN 1-904153-04-6

GRAVE-ROBBERS, CUT-THROATS AND POISONERS OF LONDON
By Helen Smith
Dive into London's criminal past and meet some of its thieves, murderers and villains.
ISBN 1-904153-00-3

DUNGEONS, GALLOWS AND SEVERED HEADS OF LONDON
By Travis Elborough
For spine-chilling tortures and blood-curdling punishments, not to mention the most revolting dungeons and prisons you can imagine.
ISBN 1-904153-03-8

THE BLACK DEATH AND OTHER PLAGUES OF LONDON
By Natasha Narayan
Read about some of the most vile and rampant diseases ever known and how Londoners overcame them – or not!
ISBN 1-904153-01-1

GHOSTS, GHOULS AND PHANTOMS OF LONDON
By Travis Elborough
Meet some of the victims of London's bloodthirsty monarchs, murderers, plagues, fires and famines – who've chosen to stick around!
ISBN 1-904153-02-X

RATS, BATS, FROGS AND BOGS OF LONDON
By Chris McLaren
Find out where you can find some of the creepiest and
crawliest inhabitants of London.
ISBN 1-904153-05-4

BLOODY KINGS AND KILLER QUEENS OF LONDON
By Natasha Narayan
Read about your favourite royal baddies and their gruesome
punishments.
ISBN 1-904153-16-X

SPIES, SECRET AGENTS AND BANDITS OF LONDON
By Natasha Narayan
Look through the spy hole at some of our greatest spies and
their exploits, to how to make your own invisible ink.
ISBN 1-904153-14-3

PIRATES, SWASHBUCKLERS AND BUCCANEERS
OF LONDON
By Helen Smith
Experience the pockmarked and perilous life of an average
London pirate and his (or her) adventures.
ISBN 1-904153-17-8

HIGHWAYMEN, OUTLAWS AND BANDITS
OF LONDON
By Travis Elborough
Take yourself back to the days when the streets of London
hummed with the hooves of highwaymen's horses and the
melodic sound of 'Stand and deliver!'
ISBN 1-904153-13-5

WITCHES, WIZARDS AND WARLOCKS OF LONDON
By Natasha Narayan
Quite simply the bizarre history of London, full of
superstition, magic and plain madness.
ISBN 1-904153-12-7

In case you have difficulty finding any Watling St books in your local bookshop, you can place orders directly through

BOOKPOST
Freepost
PO Box 29
Douglas
Isle of Man
IM99 1BQ

Telephone: 01624 836000

email: bookshop@enterprise.net